Cherry Blossoms

*Design of cherry blossoms,
branches, and a bird.*

Cherry Blossoms

Sachio Yoshioka
Supervising Editor

Original Drawings by Ichiro Tanimoto

SHIKOSHA DESIGN LIBRARY

Stone Bridge Press • Berkeley, California

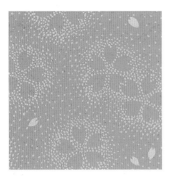

Published by
Stone Bridge Press
P.O. Box 8208
Berkeley, CA 94707
TEL 510-524-8732 • sbp@stonebridge.com • www.stonebridge.com

Book design by Fumio Shiozawa / cutcloud
http://cutcloud.net

Art direction by Art Books Shikosha Publishing Co., Ltd.

Original drawings by Ichiro Tanimoto.

Printed in China.

ISBN 978-1-933330-57-0

Cherry Blossoms

The cherry blossom—or *sakura*, as it is called in Japanese—is a symbol of cheer and hope. In Japan, where the division between the seasons is fairly distinct, the cherry blossom heralds the end of the frigid weather of winter and the onset of the warmth of spring. The day on which cherry trees are forecast to blossom is one of the highlights of the daily weather report.

The school year in Japan begins in April, just around the time the cherry trees begin to bloom. When students successfully pass a high school or university entrance exam, the feat is referred to as "a cherry tree bursting into bloom." In first grade elementary school textbooks, there is a picture of a flower at the front of the book accompanied by the script for "flower." This flower, of course, is the cherry blossom.

The cherry blossom is one of many flowers that bloom at a particular time of the year, in this case in springtime, as do the plum and peach. But Japanese have a particularly soft spot in their hearts for the cherry, unequalled by that for any other flower. In a very short period of time, the cherry trees bloom, all in unison, and then just as suddenly lose their petals. In this brief drama, the Japanese have come to see something analogous to the brevity of the span of human years and to the full-spirited way in which life should be lived.

In *Bushido: The Soul of Japan*, Inazo Nitobe (1862–1933) notes that "the *sakura* [cherry] has for ages been the favorite of our people and the emblem of our character." Later in the same book he writes, "When the delicious perfume of the *sakura* quickens the morning air, as the sun in its course rises to illumine first the isles of the Far East, few sensations are more serenely exhilarating than to inhale, as it were, the very breath of beauteous day." Few Japanese would dispute these sentiments.

There are ten basic types of cherry in Japan, with over 100 varieties thriving in the wild. From these have been produced over 300 varieties for ornamental use. The fruit is called *sakuranbō* in Japanese, and the tree is referred to in English as a Japanese cherry or flowering cherry. The cherry has always been a favorite of writers, and it figures prominently in the fable of George Washington confessing to having chopped down his father's favorite tree as well as in Chekhov's social satire *The Cherry Orchard*. In 1909 the city of Tokyo donated cherry trees to be planted along the Potomac River in Washington, D.C. These trees were of the *Somei Yoshino* variety, which is now the most widely cultivated of all cherries in Japan.

In Japan's early classical times, the flower of choice was the plum. In the *Collection of Ten Thousand Leaves* (the oldest anthology of Japanese poetry, from the seventh and eighth centuries), the plum figures in 118 poems, the cherry in 44.

In 794 the capital moved from Nara to Kyoto, marking the beginning of the 400-year-long Heian period. The southern garden of the Heian imperial palace was planted with mandarin oranges and plum trees, but when the plums failed to prosper, Emperor Kanmu (r. 781–806) recultivated the garden with mountain cherries transplanted from nearby Mt. Yoshino, a sacred mountain in the southern part of Nara. Kanmu was particularly fond of cherry blossoms, and he held lively "flower festivals" to celebrate their blossoming, accompanied by the playing of music and the penning of poetry. In time the cherry garnered a special place in the hearts of Heian aristocrats and then among the common people as well. As a result, in the most famous collection of poetry in the ninth century, *Collection of Ancient and Modern Poetry*, references to the cherry blossom far outnumber those of any other flower.

Due to the emotional appeal of its brief but beautiful life, the cherry has played a prominent role in literature and poetry, has been depicted in paintings, lacquerware, pottery and other traditional crafts, and has been featured on the stunning designs of kimono.

The present book features the work of the Kyoto kimono designer Ichiro Tanimoto. He has reproduced here the patterns of antecedent designers in a variety of styles according to his own sensibilities. Through this work, we are able to appreciate and enjoy the emotional resonances of the cherry blossom, one of the aesthetic threads that make up the fabric of Japanese culture.

How to Use This Book

The images in this book can be appreciated as they are for their intrinsic beauty. Or, if you are so inclined, you can reproduce and use them in your art or graphic design projects.

All of the images in this book can be used royalty free. They can be downloaded from the Shikosha Design Library website, which is linked to www.stonebridge.com. Many of the images are available for free download at lower resolutions for hobbyists and home users. High-resolution, high-quality versions that are intended for graphic arts professionals can be downloaded from the site for a nominal fee. Once you copy or download an image, you can use your own design tools and software to edit and manipulate it to suit your needs.

For Hobbyists and Home Users

You do not need fancy tools or software to capture or use the images in this book.

- Take this book to any photocopy service bureau and ask them to copy an image and enlarge or reduce it, in black and white or in color.
- Use tracing paper to capture outlines of images or parts of images that you can then fill in and recolor to your liking.
- If you have a decent close-up lens on your camera, take photographs and reprint them as often as you like; this works even better if you have a digital camera hooked up to an inexpensive inkjet printer at home.
- If you are artistically inclined yourself, you can freely redraw the images, using them for inspiration as you explore your own themes and develop your own designs.

For Graphic Arts Professionals

If you are a graphic arts professional you are probably familiar with using computer software to manipulate, re-color, resize, crop, and otherwise transform both line art and grayscale or color images. Here we introduce three basic techniques using Adobe Photoshop CS—solarization, adding color to black and white images, and changing image color. Photoshop is not the only software that offers these tools, and of course there are many other ways that you can use downloaded images to achieve your ends.

Throughout this book, cmyk values are given adjacent to images for reference. You can of course change these color values as desired, or use them to create matching or complementary colors. Running heads throughout indicate the types of effects displayed, including solarization and colorization and colorized solarization. The effect is usually accompanied by the original image or artwork, with the original sometimes smaller or larger than the effect depending on visual interest.

SOLARIZATION

Solarization is one type of effect you can apply to photos. In general, solarization results when you purposely overexpose film as it's developing to invert the brightness or color of one part or all of a photo. Solarization uniquely gives the sense of subtly stacking film positives and negatives on top of one another. Here, we'll use a tone curve to recreate this effect, then freely alter the image even more.

First, open the original image. Then use the Curves function to adjust the image's tones. Make a curve like that in (A), and the original image will change as shown in (B), displaying the solarization effect. The steeper you make the angle of the curve line, the more intense the solarization will become. Conversely, the gentler the curve line, the gentler the solarization. See (C).

By using the Curves panel to set tones, you'll be able to play with the look and feel more effectively than you would using the Solarization filter alone. By selecting the Freehand button on the Curves panel and experimenting with various values, you can create an even greater variety of solarization effects. See (D, E).

ADDING COLOR TO BLACK AND WHITE IMAGES

To precisely color in an outline, use the method below:

1. Connect and close any segments whose lines or borders are incomplete.

Use a drawing tool or, if you have one, a pen tablet. Examine the image carefully. If there are broken lines around the areas you want to color in separately from the background, draw a line or lines to extend them to the margins or to connect and

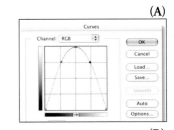
(A)

(B)

(C)

(D)

(E)

Examples of solarization.

close them. You do this so that when you click on an area with the Magic Wand tool the selection does not extend to where it is not wanted. This job can be rather time-consuming depending on the original image.

2. Make a separate layer for the outlines only.
Select only the lines around the areas to be colored in. Copy this selection onto a new layer (the "line" layer). (You can make the result cleaner using the Level Correction or Defringe functions.)

3. Make a layer for coloring.
In the line layer select the transparent, non-line areas. Copy this selection into a new layer (the "coloring layer") beneath the line layer. Use the Fill function to color the selection white. (If you enlarge the selection slightly before filling, you won't leave any area uncolored.)

4. Color freely.
In the coloring layer, activate Lock Transparent Pixels. Use the Magic Wand tool, the Paint Bucket tool, or any of the brushes to apply color to the image any way you like.

Adding color to black and white images

Create additional variations by changing the color of the image outlines. If you lock transparency when coloring, the color won't go outside the lines, and your image will have a clean look.

CHANGING COLORS IN AN IMAGE
There are many ways to change colors, but here is the most basic. Open the original image. In the Adjustments menu select Hue/Saturation. Move any of the sliders to change the color.

To change only part of the image, first select the area you wish to change, then adjust the color using the sliders.

Changing color in an image as a result of moving the Adjustments sliders.

Examples of the types of projects that can be made using the designs and patterns in this book.

Applications

There is no limit to what you can do with the images and designs in this book. You may, for example, just use a small piece of a design as a part of a logo or an understated decorative motif on a greeting card. Or you can take an entire design and expand it into a wall-size mural to decorate a hallway or bathroom or ceiling.

The designers of this book have intentionally taken the original artworks and manipulated them in various ways to demonstrate the possibilities and especially the surprising results when colors and images are flipped, tiled, or otherwise manipulated. What began as a fairly standard Asian representational motif now becomes a thoroughly modern and almost abstract rendering that still suggests an Asian aesthetic but is now charged with a modern sensibility. The color changes and manipulations in this book are just examples. If you download the images yourself, you will be able to explore many more possibilities than can possibly be shown here.

PROJECT IDEAS

Below are some possible uses for the images in this book.

- Fine artworks
- Stencils and rubber stamps
- Menus
- Web page graphics
- Posters
- Tattoos and henna body painting
- Bookplate designs
- Architectural and sculptural elements
- Picture frames
- Collages
- Greeting cards
- Fabric designs
- Lampshades
- Signs
- Quilts, embroidery, and beading
- Scrapbooks
- Cell-phone covers
- Mosaics and tilework
- Cake decorations
- Logos and letterheads

LOGOS AND LETTERHEADS

Printing on different shades of paper will produce different effects. Try using textured paper like Japanese *washi* in your inkjet printer to create antiqued designs with subtle surface qualities. Such prints are often suitable for framing on their own and can be an inexpensive and stylish way to decorate your personal space.

| Colorized Solarization of Facing-Page Image

| Solarization of Facing-Page Image

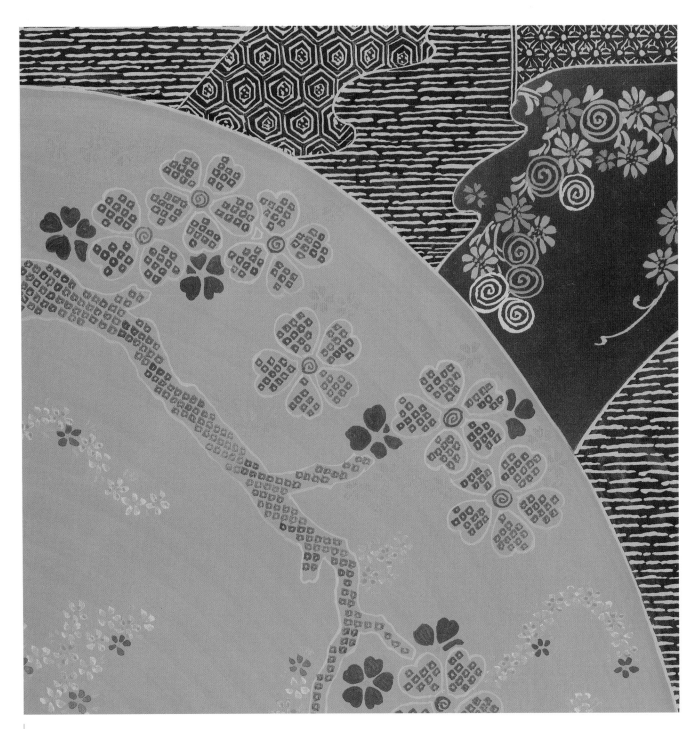

| Solarization of Facing-Page Image

| Original Image (*top*) with Solarization

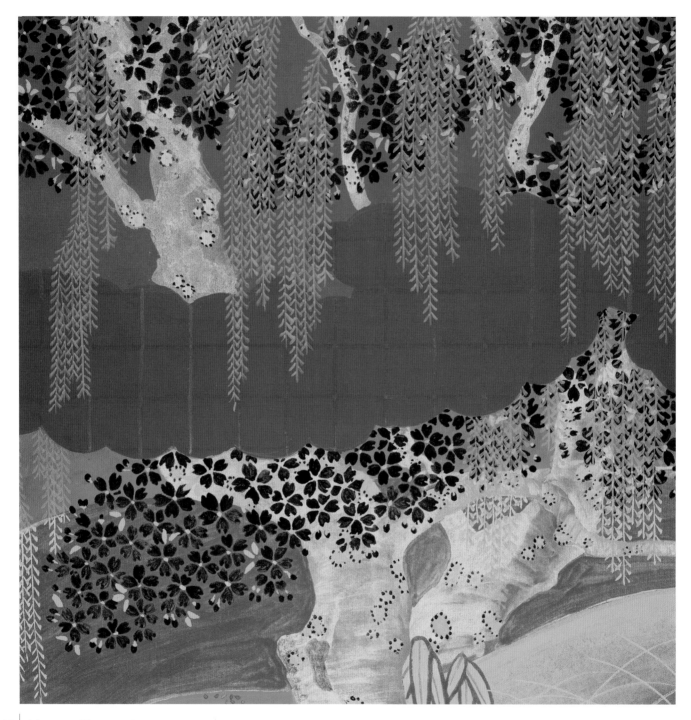

| Solarization of Facing-Page Image

| Line Art Based on Facing-Page Image

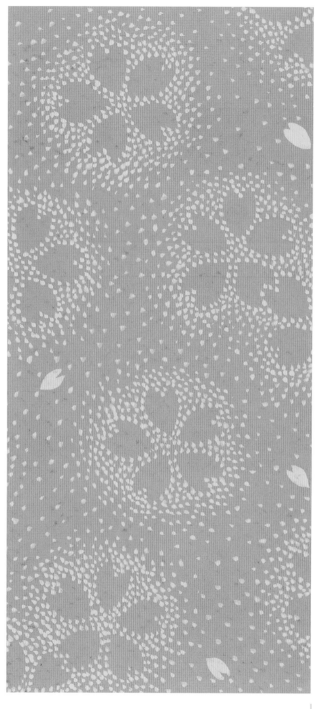

| Original Image

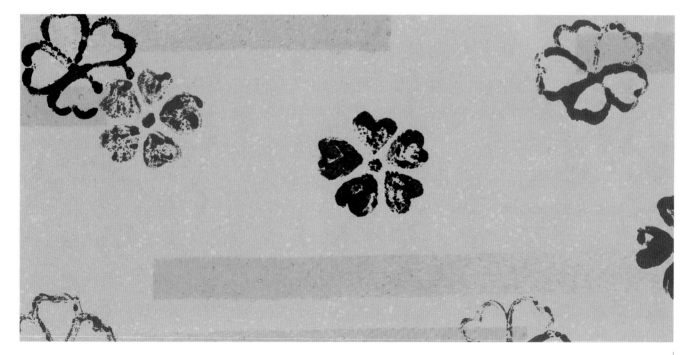

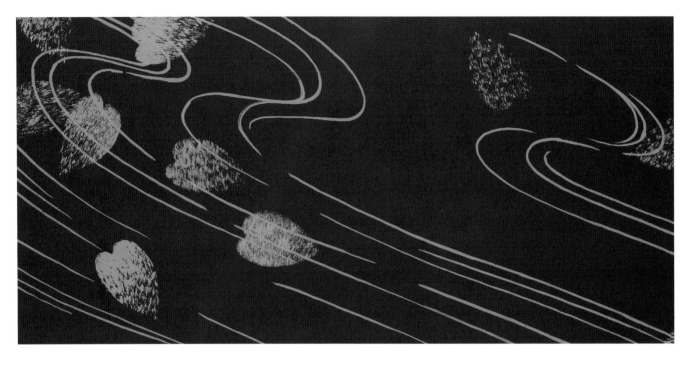

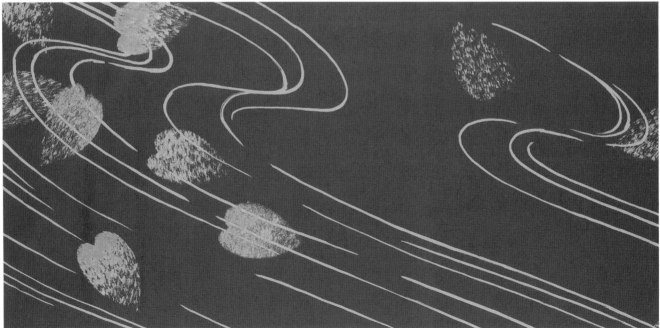

| Original Image (*top*) with Solarization

Original Image (*top*) with Solarization

| Original Image (*right*) with Solarization

Original Image (*right*) with Solarization | 45

M : 40
Y : 70

C : 50
Y : 100

M : 80
Y : 35

C : 100
Y : 100

C : 90
M : 80

C : 35
Y : 40

C : 80
Y : 100

Colorization of Facing-Page Image

| Original Image

C : 100
M : 100

M : 90

C : 60
Y : 100

Y : 20

C : 85
M : 70

C : 100
M : 100

M : 30
Y : 100

Y : 45

C : 100
Y : 50
:

M : 15
Y : 100

C : 80
M : 30
K : 30

M : 90
Y : 70
K : 10

M : 20

M : 100
Y : 100

C : 50
M : 60

M : 10
Y : 30

M : 20

M : 50
Y : 50

C : 50
M : 80

C : 100
M : 70
K : 70

C : 70
Y : 30
K : 20

C : 100
M : 70
Y : 40

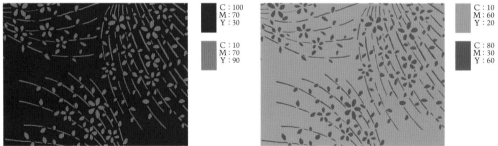

C : 100
M : 70
Y : 30

C : 10
M : 70
Y : 90

C : 10
M : 60
Y : 20

C : 80
M : 30
Y : 60

58 | Original Image with Colorization

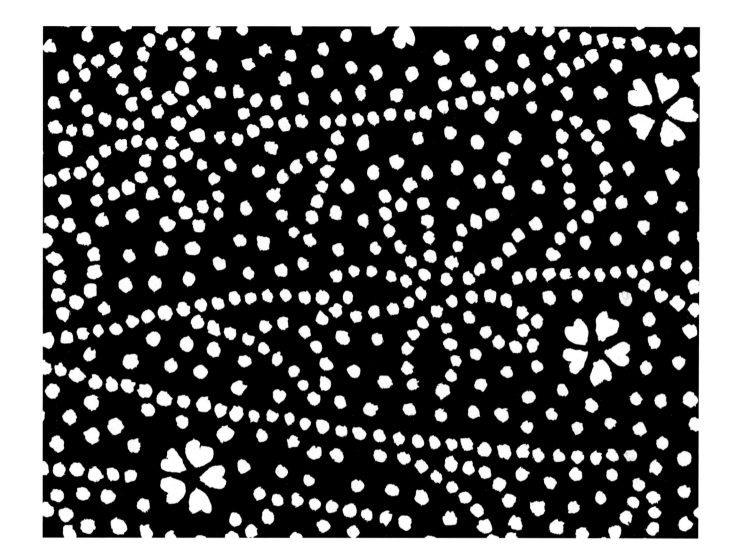

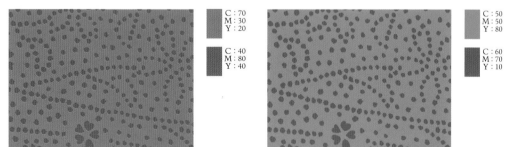

C : 70
M : 30
Y : 20

C : 40
M : 80
Y : 40

C : 50
M : 50
Y : 80

C : 60
M : 70
Y : 10

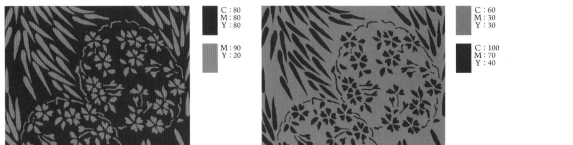

	C : 80
	M : 80
	Y : 80

| | M : 90 |
| | Y : 20 |

	C : 60
	M : 30
	Y : 30

	C : 100
	M : 70
	Y : 40

| Original Image with Colorization

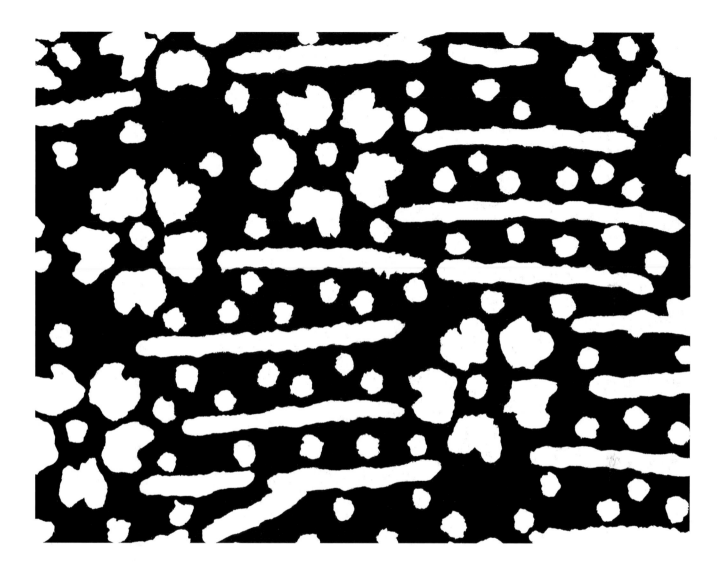

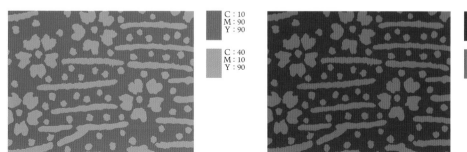

C : 10
M : 90
Y : 90

C : 40
M : 10
Y : 90

C : 100
M : 80
Y : 30

C : 10
M : 90
Y : 100

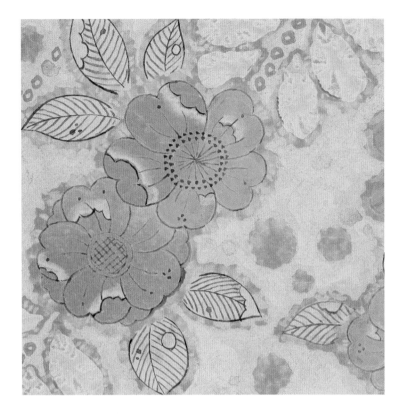

M : 40
Y : 45
K : 10

M : 90
Y : 35

Y : 90
K : 10

Solarization and Colorization of Facing-Page Image

M : 85
Y : 100

M : 100
Y : 100
K : 55

C : 100
Y : 65

M : 50
Y : 65

C : 20
M : 75
Y : 60
K : 70

C : 85
M : 30
Y : 90
K : 85

C : 65
M : 20
Y : 100
K : 40

C : 100

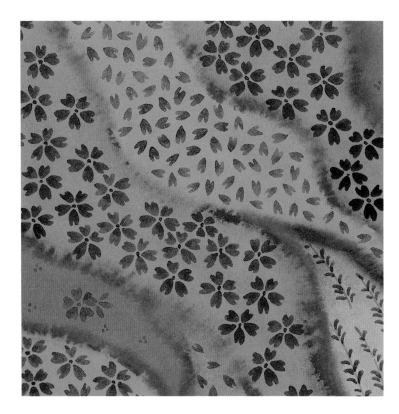

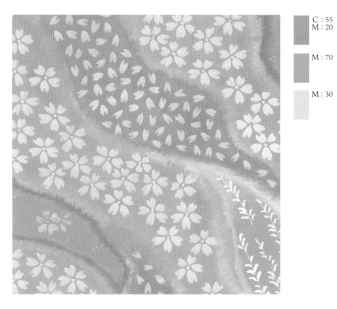

C : 55
M : 20

M : 70

M : 30

Solarization and Colorization of Facing-Page Image

C : 100
M : 30
Y : 100

C : 80
M : 20
Y : 25

M : 100

C : 50
M : 70
K : 45

M : 90
Y : 100

C : 15
M : 30
Y : 50

C : 60
M : 100
Y : 40

C : 100
M : 100
Y : 80

C : 60
M : 20
Y : 35

M : 30
Y : 100

M : 90
Y : 80
K : 85

M : 90

M : 40
Y : 75

C : 100
Y : 100
K : 10

C : 95
M : 100
Y : 100

Y : 80
M : 100

C : 100
M : 50
Y : 100

M : 50
Y : 100

C : 100

M : 40

| Colorization of Facing-Page Image

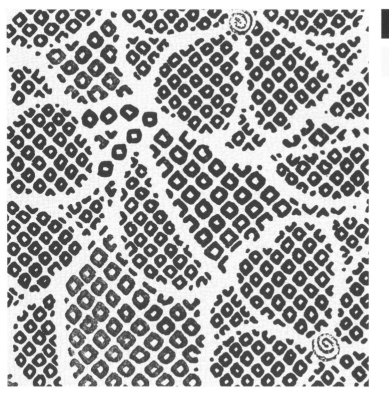

C : 50
M : 100
Y : 100

M : 5
Y : 20

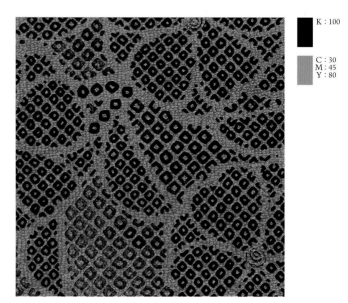

K : 100

C : 30
M : 45
Y : 80

C : 10
M : 100
Y : 90

M : 60
Y : 20

C : 75
M : 100

C : 100
M : 70
Y : 30

C : 40
M : 20
Y : 90

C : 10
M : 80
Y : 100

K : 100

M : 75
Y : 25

C : 50
Y : 100

M : 100
Y : 100

C : 80
M : 35

Y : 90

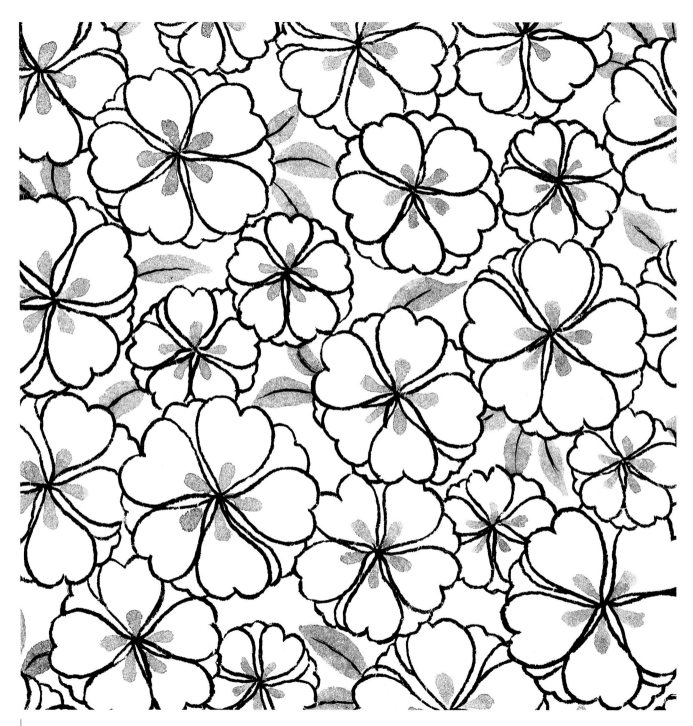

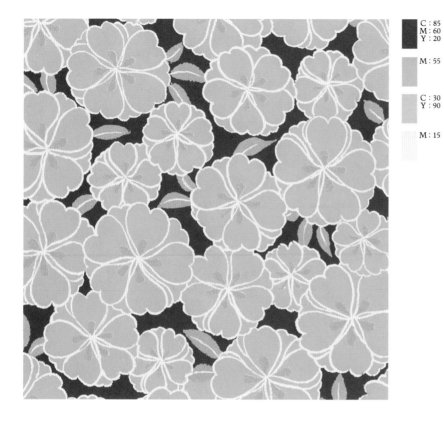

C : 85
M : 60
Y : 20

M : 55

C : 30
Y : 90

M : 15

C : 30
M : 65
Y : 80

C : 60
M : 15

C : 5
M : 10
Y : 100

C : 30

Solarization of Facing-Page Image

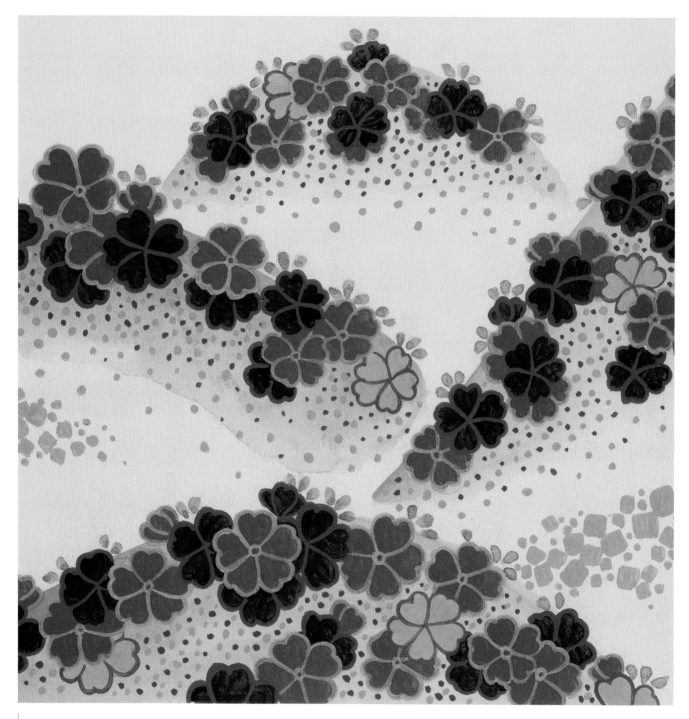

| Solarization of Facing-Page Image

Original Image (*right*) with Solarization

Original Image (*right*) with Solarization | 93

| Original Image (*right*) with Solarization

| Sword Guards with Cherry Blossoms Designs

| Original Image

C : 30
M : 25
Y : 20

C : 45
M : 100
Y : 70

Colorization and Solarization of Facing-Page Image

C : 90
M : 100

M : 5
Y : 30

M : 60
Y : 100

Y : 100
K : 30

| Original Image with Colorization

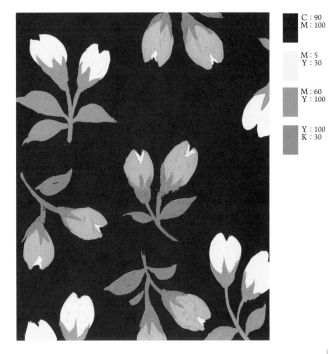

C : 90
M : 100

M : 5
Y : 30

M : 60
Y : 100

Y : 100
K : 30

Solarization of Facing-Page Image

M : 55
Y : 100

M : 20
Y : 10

M : 100
Y : 100

C : 80
M : 35
Y : 10

C : 90
M : 100

C : 100
Y : 50

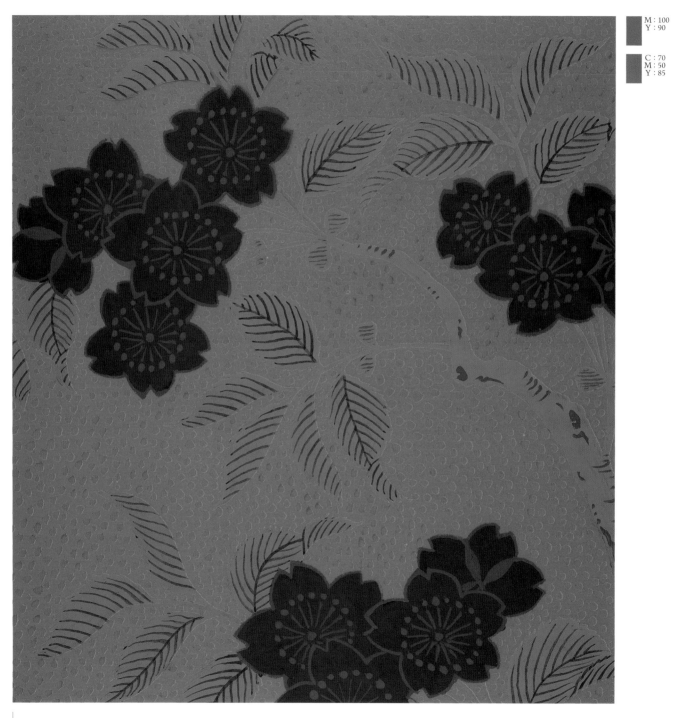

M : 100
Y : 90

C : 70
M : 50
Y : 85

Solarization of Facing-Page Image

C : 50
M : 40

M : 90
Y : 70

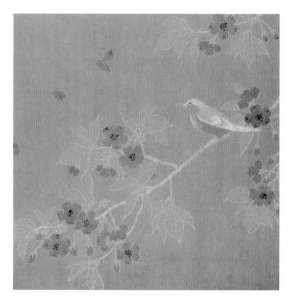

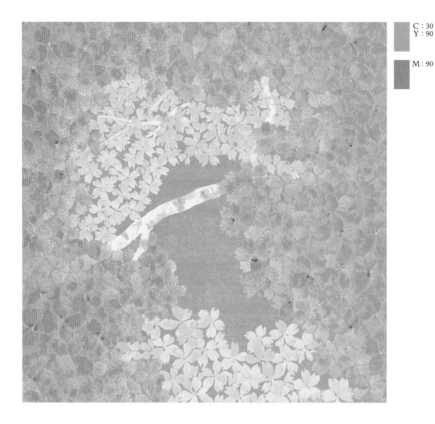

C : 30
Y : 90

M : 90

Y : 100

M : 70
K : 70

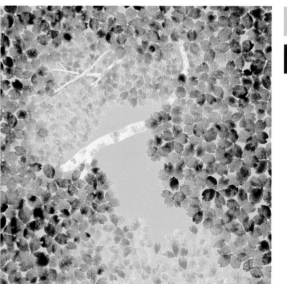

118 | Solarization of Facing-Page Image